AF442384

with concern for how words land in the body

a discography & mythobiography

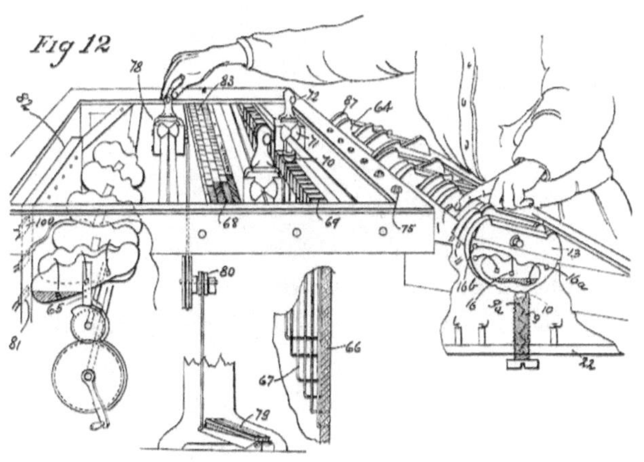

April Pameticky

Spartan
Press

Spartan Press

Kansas City, Missouri
spartanpresskc@gmail.com

Copyright © April Pameticky 2026
First Edition: 1 3 5 7 9 10 8 6 4 2
ISBN: 979-8-89975-040-3
LCCN: 2026937592

Cover art: *Three Women* by Pablo Picasso
Title page image: *Diagram for Instrument of Light and
    Color Play,* U.S. Patent Office
Author photo: Tye Pameticky

Acknowledgments:

middling paper, 2nd place, theme, kac writing contest, 2024

thursday in the shadow of kesoo, honorable mention, free
    verse, kac writing contest, 2024

salt, 1st place, narrative, kac writing contest, 2024

you dreamed so hard it felt like permanence, honorable
    mention, narrative kac writing contest, 2024

the entire collection was a semi-finalist for the birdy poetry
    prize from meadowlark books

poems that have been displayed at the Wichita Art Museum
    2023-2024
        mary
        mad baby
        we mothers and sisters

circe, wichita public library big read celebration 2023

i reach through the screen to touch your face, a pandemic
    collection for the wichita public library, 2022

day 2 of moderna vaccine, a pandemic collection for the
    wichita public library, 2022

a moth triptych, in collaboration with Irma Puškarević at
GAZE: Power and Politics April 13-May 24, 2023, Mark Arts

Table of Contents

instructions before reading

listen, linda. presumptuous of me, i know, to write out some instructions for you, though i know you'll do whatever you want. it's a ride, this catalog of poems, and maybe i have some advice:

1. you could read this like an 80s choose your own adventure novel. do you remember those, linda? at the bottom of the page would be a choice: "to follow patrick on his journey to slay the dragon, turn to page 85. to go on your OWN adventure, turn to page 93." someone was always trying to read those straight through. ugh. linda.

2. this isn't a media-free zone. let's not pretend our phones aren't attached to our hands.

so much of this collection is in dialog with something else. there are songs, artwork, and liner notes sprinkled throughout. scan the qr codes. you could look up these things before, during, or after reading. whatever your flavor, linda. it's your ride. these poems don't exist outside of their counterparts. they're reflections of better works. this collection isn't meant to be a high fidelity situation either [have you seen that cusack movie, linda? the conceit is that he tells his autobiography by the songs he was listening to at each particular point in his life]. this ain't that.

it's about who am i when i see that art, hear that song,
experience that moment. do i ever get to be that person
again? will I recognize myself in that moment later?
what version of myself do i get to be when that song is
playing and when it's over?

who do you get to be when you read it, linda? no
judgment. i hope someone somewhere is reading this
in a bathtub. careful you don't drop your phone in the
water.

just know that I wrote this book in gratitude for all
the lindas and karens and poets and artists and guitar
players and buskers and readers and lovers.

thank you.

want to just skip ahead to the end? Turn to page 90

*every time i thought i'd got it made, it seemed the taste was not
so sweet. so I turned myself to face me, but I've never caught a
glimpse of how the others must see the faker. i'm much too fast.*

-david bowie

special thanks

to molly mcferson and the wichita art museum;

to kristen beal & mina estrada of harvester arts;

to linzi garcia;

and to tye, leia, & mj.

an ingredient list

we,
me in all my various forms,
all of the innards and all of the outards,
we are a miracle of alchemy and evolution,
el shaddai and vienna,
inadequacy and unworthiness,
star dust and volcano ash.

we are hopelessness and laser-burned-uterus,
aching feet and sore left hipbone.

we are cotton-candy joy and fresh-cut grass
and rich soil and anglican choir,
crouching inner child,
a shadow self of lust and malaise,
dust and enterprise,
ambition and failure.

we are future selves and future deaths
and olive oil heating in pan.

we are so many stories we have read
and will read
and will read again,
stories we tell ourselves
and stories we've heard.

we are constantly reinvented narrative,
a personal mythology spelled
to smell like cinnamon and bananas.

made myself mythical*

in the springtime, you will roll in new bloom grass
until your body is covered in itches and chigger bites.

your clothes will be stained red-dirt brown
and smeared with green streaks.

you will lie in the starlight,
count the constellations you know,

name the ones you don't,
bask in moonlight and cicadas.

you will grow and push past your skin,
slough away winter's cells,

wash the mud from your mouth,
admire the delicate transparency of your wings.

when you stand, your feet will grasp in the way of hands,
pull blooms from stems,

feed your hunger and your empty hull,
and you will love the saccharine sting of bitter smiles,

and bash in the heads of your enemies that walk silently
    inside you.

* from "daffodil" by florence + the machine

**after listening to dancers discuss how words
land in the body***

**with special thanks to mina estrada and the podcast benevolent instruction*

you realize that you have always only halfway
liked the space between your skeletal frame and galaxies.

that you've never thought so hard about the articulation
    of toe and tongue.

that some live in their body in joy and in sorrow, married
    to movement.

while you've resented and punished your body
for not being tall enough,
strong enough,
thin enough,
smooth enough.

you've waited your whole life to make friends
with your fingers,
your scapula,
your vulva,
your knee,

to know your elbow as a dancer knows her breath,
to curve into the sunlight and sway in the rain.

**with special thanks to mina estrada and the podcast benevolent instruction*

forward fold

sliding down,
        vertebrae bones crackle,   reach

            for phalanges and   metatarsals,

            eyes close to silence vertigo
                    and world as reversal,
        blocked.

still breathing;

    still breathing.

compressed by folded torso,
        expansion restricted by pelvis and   thigh,

        though nothing is touching, *do we want
    fingers to touch toes*—

a gap with plenty of room for breath,

                but everything feels pressed
and sky too far away.

still breathing;

    still breathing.

                    view corralled by body and
        expectation,
                face warming to blood   rushing.

        let fingers release,
                grasp air,
                                inhale to rise,
                                        hands sweep up
                        and out
                                and over
                                        and now shoulders crackle.
        roll up the spine

                feel feet leave floor in flight for a moment

        spanning forever and   never.

liner note 1:

my mother, firstborn of german catholics, met and
fell in love with her second husband in 1976. she
can't remember the day they married, but she does
remember the peasant blouse she wore, knows they
said vows in tahlequah.

she graduated with her degree and her husband and
she fiercely wanted a baby. me.

in the retelling, she will always insist this fiercely, the
story more fierce upon repetition, that while other
things crumbled, she was so fiercely glad of me.

when I was a child, i believed her.

as an adult i started to realize that things were
impossible, that she moved in with his family when
i came because there was no place else, because she
couldn't go back home to her own parents, felt she
had too many failures, and maybe i would be just one
more. that somehow she had a second husband and
no real job and had decided law school couldn't work,
and so she emphasizes that i was a choice she wanted
to make.

this is not the story the way she would tell it. when
does it stop being her story and start being mine?

memory is a faulty, made-up thing, a blanket folded
and twisted and stuffed in the far back. we reconstruct,
and reknit, and refold, smooth away wrinkles with our
hands, and the result is that our mind tells us whatever
we need to know in the now to support our survival.
we forget what we don't need. rescript what we know.
and no one is better at rewriting her own narrative than
my mother.

and me.

beige walks into a bar, draft 3

we have never known a story
where the hero wears beige this seems insurmountably
     important
to us that morally ambiguous gray and
decisive black receives far too much credit.

we argue over whether buff
is somehow ethically superior to teal,
that at least teal seems able to make decisions.
we say that it is right and true
for a wall to be any of these iterations:

fawn
buff
sand(y)
camel
mushroom

all things I would rather not put in my mouth.

that it is right and true always and everywhere
for beige to be background but never foreground,
never focal point.
neutral becomes murder,
is a coward,
and that we'd never trust
a beige walking down the street.

the sound beige makes
is a soft exhalation that sighs past the vocal cords
but never speaks substance.

salt

> *—but lot's wife, behind him, looked back, and she became a pillar of salt.*
> genesis 19:26

1

she grabs the plastic shaker from the edge of the
orange formica table, the corner booth a classic
green vinyl in the waffle house off i35, grabs the
white shaker before anyone can say no, shimmies a
pinch into the palm of her hand, glances around for
judgment or censure, then licks from stem to stern all
the tiny granules.

2

we sit in the heat of jet, oklahoma, july 1986, sand
and grit grimed under my fingernails, my pouch
already full of hourglass crystals, and i don't want to
do this anymore, this terrible trip to mark my summer
birthday. i want to go to Big Splash but this is more
"educational," and i would honestly learn so much
when I gathered my very own state rose rocks in
the Great Salt Plains. in a little while i will melt into
the thirsty red dirt, melt into the cracks of iron and
sage, but this is before that, when we are still digging,
endless scooping motions, hands carved into claws,
carving scars in the red dirt.

3
when I am days from my 18th in 1995,
my stepbrother will roll his truck
on old hubbard road between
blackwell and ponca city,
and i will lose the only other person in existence
who knows what it is like to be a child
in his father's house.

he won't mean to do it,
has lived so many choices by impulse, even down to
     this one,
but it will happen and he will die.

but, for right now, we are quibbling over whether that
     jar full of white granules is salt or sugar.

we have specific containers for these things,
specific and carefully labeled containers,
but we have no idea what is in that jar
because mom helped a church lady
clean out her cabinets.
i dare him to just taste it,
just tump the glass sideways
into his mouth and take a big gulp.

so he does, a mouthful plopping faster than he can slide,

all this is in his mouth,
he erupts, spews white sand across the kitchen,

his face screwing up,
a contorted kissing spasm.

i laugh until
i taste salt tears.

want to re-read that yoga poem? turn to 6.

how soon is now*

you were 14 when you first swallowed a dragon,
learned to breathe fire
and eat coal
and welcome heat
and sweat
and no more tears.
when you first believed you could see auras,
and knew the bastards in the room
with claws for hands
and blood on their teeth.
when you first decided
that hate was better than love,
and you would not clench your fists in secret anymore,
would not shut your mouth,
but would smile with fang and forked tongue.
when you first resolved to grow large enough
to devour all your enemies
with a belly full of salt.

**from the song of the same name by the smiths*

church ladies

today the church ladies will include you on an email
chain you don't wish to be part of, will invite you
to a saturday day of service, and you will not want
to, but you can't kick puppies and you don't want
to disappoint, so you will just not answer—ignore
it like the daily one from best buy that you haven't
figured out how to unsubscribe from—will tell
yourself you received this email along with any
other number of church ladies because they are
attempting the scatter-gun approach for volunteers,
and it's not like you have anything else do saturday
[well you do have other things you would rather
do, and you don't want to do this], so you passively
quit, ignore, filter to junk folder, pretend they never
even asked you, even though it will bother you that
they never even ask.

where my foodies at? for gingersnaps, 38. for awkward
family conflict, 59 or 74 .

liner note 2:

i could tell my mother's story. i've heard her tell it
enough it's become the background vocals to my own
jazz hands.

but this is my story for once, told in my own broken
and imperfect way, and I will choose to hold to my
own telling despite the mess i will make of it. because
none of it could truly all occur should I spread it out
chronologically in a fact-checked historical timeline. like
pulp fiction. without the cocaine. or john travolta.

just trauma-brain and pop-psychology references.

perhaps that's part of why i'm so hesitant to tell my
own life in anything other than poem and metaphor.
because the story she tells is hers, not ours.

it's hard to revisit the places that hurt, to own the
landscape that led me here and made me harsher and
less maternal than I yearn to be. mother hunger. mom
guilt. my daughters deserve to know me beyond the life
and mythology their father and i have created.

i am twins carrying my broken shadow, half of me
crumpled and folded in the back, my other half
walking in the light.

mary*

it's her hands curled gently in her lap,
fingers lax in soft surrender.

she sat tense for hours,
until she gave up the head tilt, gave up the fear,

gave up her long to-do list of all the things
appropriate wives do,

drained tension like water down the slope of
    shoulders,
sat still on her stool,

sat still her breath falling into cupped hands,
a loose grasp of nothing,

to spill on her tucked bare feet below.

**from mrs. mary hallock greenewalt (1903) by tomas eakins (1844-1916),
permanent collection of the wichita art museum*

liner note 3:

there's something about mary…

for at least a week, I sat across from mary's painting,
avoided her gaze, the awkward neck tilt. then i leaned
in, started to talk to her like she and i were having tea
(i don't even like tea; what a waste of caffeine), but
mary and i started to hang out.

go ahead and look at the painting, linda. see the
curious head tilt, the curl of hands in her lap.

turns out, mary was a trained concert pianist and
genius, inventing a patented machine that would
represent sound with color called a *nourathar.*

i spent years wanting to play piano, studied for an
aggregate total of 2 years—i say aggregate because at
no given time was i allowed to pursue piano study for
more than 6 months at a time, although they did offer
a piano class at the magnet where I went to school, all
of us in rows of electric pianos, all of us learning the
same "minuet in g" so that we could play in tandem
at the end of the year, and my fingers still contain the
muscle memory to play that song, although I can no
longer read bass clef and i'm not sure I ever even saw
the sheet music to that song. music lives in our bones.

i have told mary, mrs. greenewalt, to play something
soothing, but she just looks at me and reminds me that
she's not spotify, and I'm chagrined to remember that
she's a person with sore hands and fierce ideas about
color and sound. she gets fed up with the frivolous,
and that includes me sometimes.

is there a cream for that?

my life-long love affair with sunshine
has left a map of indonesian islands across my
    cheekbones
and continents across my brow,

there is no makeup that conceals i'm midlife,
that i don't actually like to exercise, find it a bore,
so i grow softer and oddly rigid.

i must resist buying more products,
more miracle creams,
more gimmicks to slim down my waist.

nothing will give me smaller ankles when all the
    muscle
to move this body is contained in a 22-inch inseam.
i will never have long calf muscles.

i know that this is an embarrassment of riches,
that I can move, am healthy, nothing is broken,
but but but

i didn't expect that my body would never be the
    same body
from day to day, that I would have to reintroduce
    myself
to my own toes each day, my own knees,

that sometimes my body would betray me and hurt me
    and ultimately let me down,
or maybe I'm letting this body down,
that i've been given a ferrari and I've chosen to treat it
    like a fiat.

*In the mood for more dying? try 44. want to feel
a little uncomfortable? 51.*

circe

she moves through sand and wave,
spoken word and power,
witch—
endless.
Were we to meet her
on the subway
eating her mortal sandwich,
away from her isle,
we would discuss the weft and warp,
the finishing,
to be a mother,
to lose and hate.
but mostly we would talk
about gods and lovers
and the fine art of dying.

thursday in the shadow of kesoo*

like sunshine through eyelids
like warmth and safety
like movement through tall grass
like matchstick just before the flare
like soft touch in darkness
like cracked pepper
or saltwater brine
or smoky bourbon
like the memory of breakfast
like humming without melody
just the confirmation that i heard you
like marconi union while sitting on a backless bench
in the middle of wichita art museum
like that time we stretched out on the sidewalk
to feel the heat come up through our clothes
like the steering wheel sat too long in the sun
like that time I told her I would never do that to her
as it was done to me,
like a vow.

** "kesoo" (1977) by artist natvar bhavasar (1934-present), permanent collection of the wichita art museum*

coyote

we're lying in the divots our bodies and time have
    created
on our parallel sides of the mattress.

i can hear the weighted stillness from his side of the bed,
the measured breath,
awful effort to pretend to sleep.

he stirs at the sound of the train a quarter-mile down
    the road,
horn calling out to warn travelers from crossing over,

and then the coyotes call,
subtle *yipping* and laughter,
echo back to the train from the pack denning
on the eastern shore of our subdivision pond.

he moves closer,
over the geographic divide of hummock and down
    comforter,
curls me into his space.
we hold and listen to the howls,
the cool night broken by song.

here we dwell in mess and beauty

that moment when my youngest makes her way to my
    room,
hugs me,
tells me it's time to get up because dad made breakfast.

when my oldest flops down next to me on the couch
    because her phone
finally ran out of juice,
and she just wants to know what I'm doing.

when a poem finally comes together,
finally arrives where it's going to land
and i can say
it is done.

that moment when he reaches across to grasp
    my hand,
asks me if there's anything i need.
and there's nothing i need in that moment but this.

liner note 4

so let me start with the beginning as it was told to me.

my father had dark wavy hair that he tamed with a
blow-dryer, a thick dark mustache, crooked teeth
he refused to fix for fear it would mess with his
embouchure. he was a musician, a sax player, part
choctaw, and apparently quite charismatic when he
talked politics.

he liked smart women, even when they completely
disagreed with him—as my mother assures me she
did. of their courtship, i know nothing beyond this. i
know he was married before and that he had a son. he
collected wives and children like my kids collect rocks.

they divorced before my first words. my mother
always reminds me that his family supported us
through my first year, that she lived with them and
tried to make a life for us.

after their divorce, my mother's life moved on, and
while i did actually see my father over the years, what
i remember is scattered and disjointed.

he drove a fiat. i remember thinking that his car was
exciting because it was a convertible and seemed tiny
and fast. we'd spend weekend visits with parts strewn
across his parking space next to his car at his apartment
complex.

later, we'd spend the evening listening to jazz on the
radio, and he'd get his sax out and play along, the
magical sound curling around us, me curled on the
couch waiting for the midnight show of *dr.* who
        to start
on the public access channel.

i can remember the way smoke would curl from his
mouth as he talked, sometimes leaving the cigarette to
bounce along his lip—a trick i learned in college,
        to talk
around a cigarette, the smoke stinging my eyes.

she falls around me*

1

i sing a song of myself,
reconstruct puzzles from different boxes,
a hartigan of brushstrokes,
an image that's large-part make-believe
and small parts album covers from 90s rock bands.

2

it is when satan is lord of the airways
 over all secular music,
all music not praising god and his holy son jesus,
all music is in satan's service.

he was part of the angelic choir,
did you know?
a heavenly host.

3
i
attend church,
raise hands,
babble in tongues,
and listens to nirvana on my walkman™.

this is not a poem so much as a swallow,
a fundie's love sonnet without form.

4

i listen to T95
in secret,
walk slowly the 1.8 miles between
my high school and rental on woodchuck,
walk and listen, day after day.

i would roll the FM dial back to KLUV
before I opened the door to that house where

he has been watching and waiting,
could see me from the crosswalk,
my sax banging against my leg with each stop,
as he listened to the police scanner
and smoked cigarettes.

he checks my walkman™,
checks my backpack.

this is not a poem so much as a confessional.

he says he knew satan personally
and would recognize him anywhere.

5

my daughters don't quite understand how radio works
yet:

skip this song, mom, they say;
they don't get the tacit submission,

that you had to listen to whatever the dj chose,
and is it any wonder I became a dj for a little while,
picked my own songs in devil-worshiping glee?
constantly mix and remix the playlist of my life.

this is not a poem so much as a mix-tape.

6
it was that time when we are walking,
trying to decide if we are ledbetter kids
or in bloom,

i'm pretty sure there's no reason
we can't be both
except we're apparently picking sides
for a war i didn't know was happening.

i can't tell if he's watching me,
can see me,
and so it doesn't matter in this moment

during this poem that is not a poem
but feels more like I'm still sneaking around,
listening to my life on my walkman™.

*from glycerine (1994), sixteen stone,
bush wondering if it's all 90s alt
arbage? try 44.*

grace and i

for grace hartigan

might not have been friends
as much as i would've wanted to be friends.

she would've found me too conciliatory,
too midwest nice,
a *care-bear* as irma would say,

and though i would love to watch her paint,
in fury,
in haze,
she would find me distracting,
would shout at me to stop asking her to explain,
and she would finally tell me
that I apologize too much for taking up space.

**east river drive (1957) by grace hartigan (1922-2008), permanent
collection of the wichita art museum*

we have explained this all to her several times

star-fish-stretched-out on beige stainmaster plus,
$2.38 / square foot, chosen for its versatility and the
unbearable lightness of being beneath our feet and
beneath our notice until something spills,

my nose deep in the pile attempting to sniff out cat
urine or dog vomit or literally spilt milk from the
12-year-old despite numerous admonishments that
food and drink stay in the kitchen.

we have gone over this section of carpet with the
shampoo hoover twice already with the patented
carpet detergent in *lemon citron*, and the ghost of
soiled padding lingers in the memory of the tiny hairs
in my nose.

we will not cut this square away to replace only this
1 foot section and pretend all is well beneath our
patchwork quilt of carpeting. we will pray the cat does
not discover this spot and that nothing new tips from
cups that should be in kitchens. i am deep down tired
and will stay here, sink below the wave while he lights
incense.

this one could lead you to home depot or "mad baby" on 55.
or for a palate cleanser, jump ahead to 32.

pour

she leaves the water pitcher on the counter
wide-mouthed dripping,
counter-top crowded
with flour and sugar and briny cheese.

she has left the water pitcher on the counter
instead of the crowded table
where we gather,
clustered too close
sharp elbows,
yellow cheese
egg
and breakfast toast.

she left the water pitcher on the counter,
cracked porcelain and dawn sunshine
bleaching color from wan faces,
smells crowded together
and swallows of morning milk.

** italien still life, no 2 (1930) by konrad
cramer (1888-1963), permanent
collection of the wichita art museum*

middling paper

there was that time,
because there was always that time,
where you folded in upon yourself,
emerged as an origami crane with wings
that raised and lowered as your
triangular tail raised and lowered.

you were paper masticated and swallowed,
chewed back into pulp and returned to a furious form,
a seed of flight, a bad haircut on a saturday night date,
you were in the stomach of yourself,
always hungry and devouring,
needing to soak and grow into catalpa,
broad leaves shining in the kansas swelter,
that time when summer moves into
hot blow-dryer, a fierce moist misery.

you waited for the fall fires
and setting suns
and any indication that autumn leaves
might get that brief two-week interval
to change and slide into orange and red
before dropping to
crunching carpet beneath our walking feet.

there was that time when you were something new,
something different than what you are now,

your yesterday-self not yet overlapping
with your tomorrow-self,
but just a middling newness that felt like a fresh piece
    of paper.

baking gingersnaps for the first time

they each scrunch noses at the smell,
thick molasses and ginger.

you promise them
they will love the flavor
once they cool,
but skepticism has wrought
new geography across sister faces.

each day is a universe
we attempt to fill.

liner note 5

my mother tells me that i have my father's hands, the
same shape of cuticle, fingers exactly his, that she
spotted this remarkable likeness on the day i was born.
while both of my girls carry my stamp heavily,
neither share my hands. i am very much my mother's
daughter in looks and shape, but not in hands.

i haven't seen my father's hands since i was thirteen.

sometimes my dad would be gone for months,
wouldn't call or write or visit at all. and i would
forget him a little, remind myself that he was like
the marlborough man or magnum pi. my mom saw
little if any child-support from him. he disappeared
when my mom got married, turned back up after she
divorced, not for any romantic reason or to reconnect
with my mother, but because she would reach out to
him and remind him that he still
had a daughter.

maybe she shouldn't have.

we was an awful father. not because he hurt me; he
never did anything to me.

he barely remembered my name.

trip to the moon part 1

she speculates whether it makes sense
to build a colony there,
what with no water or air or anything fun

like colby-jack cheese.

you marvel over her six-year-old mind
that moves from belief that stars hang in the sky like
    stickers,

to knowing that the earth spins miraculously
through the primordial ooze.

"like this, momma," she says,
spinning on tiptoes,
arms outstretched,
"we spin like this."

trip to the moon part 2 is on 43, or are you ready for okgo? 34.

she's in the air*

in between molecules

                                   of   oxygen   and   carbon

dioxide

             you occupy space

well, not you but some imaginary approximation of
    what your soul might be

distended droplets

               swollen glistening bubble of self

     a very thin barrier of soapy self

all selves

         lilac slushy

we are all only an approximation of things other people
    have asked us to do

** From "Only in Dreams" by Weezer*

bones keep looking back*

today you are grass green and sky blue, taste of ramen
    with no flavor packet.

you are the ache in your left hip, ring light tilted left of
    face, shadow bleeding over nose.

you are unencumbered mouth, that thing you said to
    your daughter after you turned into your mother.

you are that thing you can't even articulate in the front
    space of your mind.

your bones keep the memory of everything you've
    ever said and done, or intended to say or do,
every childhood illness, every time someone touched
    you when you asked or didn't ask,
every slip of the tongue that transformed you into
    monster.

it all cures in your skeletal frame barely held together
    by the softening of cartilage and expectation.
half the time you're not even aware that you live in
    this body,

you're just a balloon floating, caught by string.

* from "the one moment" by okgo

the meaning of life

*is that all of this will end.**

we hide from our deaths—deny the deaths of others.
we have no clear plan beyond the immediacy of funeral
arrangements
      [and we've made of that a consumerist
       nightmare
      full of hidden fees and impossible obligations].
the business of dying is thriving.

1
she has splashed you with what is left in the bottom
   of her cup,
a cup filled with 'treated' water from the city's splash-
   pad at river side park.
memory overlaps with now as you cringe away from
   all the things
you imagine and know live within that water.

Now, in her 14-year-old-voice,
she quietly tells you over the phone that she doesn't
   really want to talk to you,
even though you've been gone for days, have kinda
   missed her snappy mouth.
there's bored teenager in her voice,
but her comment stabs deep like piss splashed on your
   face from a cup filled with chlorinated water.

you should probably write your mom an apology note.

2

when your brother died and you looked down on his
    face,
it was the first time you had seen a dead body.

you couldn't bring yourself to touch his waxy skin,
        couldn't bring yourself to look too closely at
    his unfamiliar face,
a face you truly knew all too well, but here it looked
    like a bad sketch.

when your brother died, you were still trying to decide
if he even really belonged to you,
        if you had any rights to feel any way through
    the complication
                of the quilted-ripped-stitchery that
    was family,
                        stepfather and stepbrother
    and half-sibling and cousin,

as no one now knew you here at this funeral, and others
    seemed to feel the loss more deeply.

when you felt nothing and less than nothing,
                                numb,
and it was all just theater,
        even you were theater,
                and that's what death is at first:
                        theater with barely
    memorized lines.

today you give yourself permission to bring your
    brother
with you everywhere you go;
you don't worry too much that you've fictionalized
who he might've been or who he might be to others,
just decide that the idea of him belongs squarely
    with you.

3
we count our losses closely, keep them privately
    away from others,
pretend they don't live inside us, that the reason the
    old so willingly go is because
they are full up, and there's no more room for anyone
    else.

* from "the one moment" by okgo

liner note 6

i had an okgo phase. it's cool. i didn't have their faces
plastered on my wall [that was nkotb, iykyk, and I
have not yet written those poems]. but their videos are
something else.

and they're on my *eternal-feel-good* playlist. do you
have one of those, linda?

so here's a story about poison ivy that doesn't include
dads.

i grew up in apartment complexes, mini-cities of
buildings and fake green spaces and even fake ponds
with real ducks and real duck sh*t.

my friend and i found the boundary of one green space,
and a barbed-wire fence that crossed over into a huge
empty field. all of this, the big empty field, the complex
itself, all the buildings, was tucked into the curve of
a major highway, so even though we could hear the
constant noise of traffic and big semi-trucks, the trees
were thick enough that for a few feet, we could pretend
we were in the wild wild woods.

my friend and i, i think we were about 11, we decided to
create our own fort, a hide-out, a place we could bring
books and sketchpads, and just hide from everyone else.

we found a nearly rotted wooden pallet—so we had
the barbed wire and some beautiful greenery all over
it on one side, and the pallet as a gate on the other.

we spent the entire day there. our mothers must've
been furious when we didn't come home when they
called for us. though physically we were probably
only a block or two away, we never could've heard
any shouting.

and so, it wasn't 'til dark when we finally made our
way home.

i was tired, hungry, and thirsty. i knew my mom was
mad at me, but i was totally thinking about how I was
going to go back the next day and just stretch out and
watch the sunlight through the leaves.

too bad my body, and the poison ivy i had been rolling
around in, had other ideas.

it was BAD. real bad.

my tongue swelled. i was red and itchy all over.

my mom was worried—i didn't have flesh on my
body that wasn't raised in a red rash or itchy welts, not
even my butt or the tops of my feet.

it wasn't like i had rolled around naked in that poison
ivy… but i also probably didn't wash as good as i
should've in the tub—which swirled the oils from the
plant around anyway. and some folks are just unlucky
enough to be terribly sensitive to it.
it's odd. i know i was miserable, but i don't remember
it as misery.

i remember the sense of peace i had in that place,
surrounded by the green.

i remember making plans to go back.

i wish i could go back to before.

before i knew better.

i reach through the screen to touch your face

i was told once,
by someone who knew better than me,
what poetry should be,
that readers travel the lines to escape
the mechanized and
technologized anthem of the world.

to greener pastures we go.

i wonder now,
what that sage would say,
to our lcd interface,
our cameras and mics
and careful placements of digital backgrounds,
of our shares and likes and new emoticons
because we can't hug each other in the real.

we have become projections,
the hologram of our digital selves,
and we drink deeply and still thirst.

want to jump to other pandemic squander? 60.

lovely dead things

the question of whether to look down
            or just go around
has stilled our steps.

we stare and attempt to un-stare,
        look away,
                but we can't.

so we give in,
peer closer,
                lean in together,
                    brave in our collective curiosity.

we try to determine the *why* of it,
or even the *what* of it.

maybe it was a cat, you offer,
because cats are always the villains in these stories
        —cats and cars—
but today we think it was probably a cat,
and you worry that you're going
to have to explain all of this to them.

a tangle of words explaining the complexities of death
and dying and spirit are caught behind your teeth…

but, their minds have already moved on
to the popsicles waiting in the freezer at home.

firefly

he would reach down in the cicada twilight,
leaning far over,
bent in half like a rubber-band man,
would reach down with one negligible hand,
and grasp a lightning bug in the cave of his fist,
delicately hold out to me that reached hand,
now open, palm up,
and I would reach out my own hand,
waiting palm down,
and he'd smear the life of that bug across
my ring finger so that I would glow
in the massacred dusk,
glow in the twin elms of disgust and delight.

flight

you have warned her–
          as is your motherly duty to do so–
carry your own catastrophic thinking with you
     everywhere you go,
keep your own feet firmly planted on the ground.
but she wants to fly far and beyond,
so determined and so sure,
until finally you get out of her way,
love that she's braver and dumber than you,
watch her in envy as she stretches,
pulls muscles you have never used,
tastes the sky in a way that you will never know.

trip to the moon part 2

the green of my childhood
only existed
except between the uniform
apartment buildings
boasting patio decks
too small to park bikes.

thump and step of neighbors,
the soundtrack of my life.
i learned to play "heart & soul"
on an antique upright
tucked away in a 2nd story stairwell,
middle c too wet to play

all the cats we loved
adopted
gave away
to make room for so many husbands
and boyfriends who collected
quartz and tanzanite.
i am secret beige carpet stain
hidden by couch.

all the green spaces smell
of parking lot asphalt
and hot gulps of air.

liner note 7:

i know what you're thinking, linda.

where's the bowie? Or prince?

listen, linda, i tried. bowie and i hang out on the regular.
his essential playlist on apple music is permanently
streaming on my phone.

but every time i hear *ground control to major tom*, i cry.
every. damn. time.

i can't help it. it's like i'm tapping into some kind of
collective grief. didn't we all cry to hear astronaut
commander chris hadfield singing "space oddity"
from space? i have a running theory that we pack up
our societal grief whenever it becomes inconvenient,
like we just tuck it away in a holiday storage bin. but
some of us can never quite keep our bin lids closed.
things crack open and spill out. one time, jewel's 90s
hit, "foolish games," started playing on the radio,
and i had to pull the car over so that i could have a
good weep about a breakup that never even happened
to me. poets
are so annoying.

maybe I was crying over my imaginary breakup with
the goblin king.

and don't get me started on prince. without
understanding his gorgeous androgynous sexuality
at all, 9-year-old me sang the lyrics of "darling nikki"
to an understandably horrified aunt. i had no idea
what nikki was doing with that magazine, but that
song had *something.*

when prince died, i holed myself in my bathroom
for an evening and just sobbed my way through *purple
rain* on repeat.

i'm exaggerating… a little. when you're a mom, there's
no actual lock on any bathroom door that will keep
your children out. but when my oldest burst in and
then asked why I was crying, after i answered, she
said: "did you even *know* him?"

yes. i knew him. in the way we all know our favorite
artists and musicians.

so there's no poem to bowie. no answer to a prince
beat. but it wasn't for lack of trying.

*commander chris hadfield singing
"space oddity" from space*

here i come*

somewhere between childhood
and adulthood we become immeasurably concerned
with how others might watch us move through the
    world.
we temper action with fear of perception.

this could be a good thing because we don't want to
    be assholes.

we want to be liked and part of the group,

to fit in.

we forget how to run.

maybe we weren't fast enough
and never won any races.

or maybe we fell that time,

skinned our knees,

sprained an ankle,

stained our clothes beyond

baking soda and scrub brush.

or maybe we make that weird face
when we run, contorting our mouths,
and when I say run I don't actually mean run
because a lot of you fools run and love it and stay fit.
both of them,
have lost the power to run like this,

full-tilt,
no self-consciousness.

that's the fulcrum point,
the slow tilt toward dying for all of us
as we give up a little more of our own delight every day.

*from here i come (2022) by judith schaechter (1961-), permanent collection
of the wichita art museum—an approved digital image is not yet available at
the time of publishing in the online collections due to its recent acquisition by
the museum.

let us break bread together again someday

smells will swirl around us as we begin the siloing
process. politeness stiffens our walls; mealtime
etiquette will have us avoiding topics like religion or
politics except for elderly aunts who shoot well-aimed
snark, us buttoning up our coats even though we'd
planned to stay. we will carefully walk around our
ghosts. kids will shatter that, noisy and abrupt, hugs
and sticky kisses, so shy and excited to see every one
person while we hold our secrets carefully above their
heads to avoid catastrophe and spilled stuffing. we will
eat to avoid talking, eat to avoid sharing, eat to keep
our walls firm against judgment and carefully crafted
questions designed to reveal party affiliations and
sunday morning obligations, but the truth of us is
buried beneath green
bean casserole and watergate salad.

a short history of squander

things i did (or did not) do
during the covid19 pandemic*

—prescribed daily healthy activities like journaling
or walking that I only sometimes did and then never
    did, ever.

 —bought 16 tarot decks, all unique, all filling
a desperate
acquisitive
need to occupy the space-time continuum.

—cleaned toilets

—ignored other poets out of bitterness and
    resentment

—pretended to watch videos
of poets reading their work as
we reached across the pandemic divide

—counted my blessing and practiced gratitude

 —cussed out the bitch
who got to the last package of toilet paper
before me

—ate delicious things handmade and crafted by other
    people

—ate cardboard because after a while, everything
    tasted like paper

—purchased yoga pants with elastic waists
and pretended i would be doing yoga,
spontaneously,
just whenever

—burned down relationships
and set fire to my insides
(this is not a metaphor
although it could be a metaphor)

—repaired my perfectly repaired house

—did not wash a single load of laundry for 11 days
    just to see if
we all had enough clothes to survive the apocalypse

 —checked out books with interesting covers

—read books

—did not read books

—made the decision to purchase every variation
    and style of cloth mask;

washed,
ironed,
repaired
40 masks
on a weekly basis
for all members of the household

—cast spells I created after reading tarot cards
where the devil made me do it,
whatever *it* tended to be

—created an entire multi-line-mantra where
    I ultimately
just plagiarized Tina Fey:

"Bitches get shit done."

—paid for writing classes on Zoom that I did not
    attend

—watched the news

—doomscrolled for hours

—got in fights with my mother over the validity of
    masking

—quit Facebook. twice.

—stacked and restacked books with interesting covers,

only to return them to the library through
the socially-distant drive-thru
where I was forced to open the driver-side-door
because I could never park my vehicle quite close
    enough
just to hand the stack over.

—slept and overslept and underslept and
came to hate the word slept,
the past-tense of which is woke.

—learned to play guitar

—learned to bake bread

—wondered hard if we were worth saving

—submerged myself in a sensory deprivation chamber
meant to resemble the womb,
where I thought a lot about the universe inside me,
and the artificial sounds of the ocean
reminded me to inhale and exhale

 —spent approximately one million quadrillion hours
on camera speaking out to deep space
to students who were streaming *Tiger King*
while I tried to explain frederick douglass.

—developed an entire paradigm of thinking
related to psychic energy

and the rate-of-exchange
versus the cost-benefit-ratio
of remote teaching.

—traced the ghosts of our former selves
sitting like layers of paint over our faces.

—told everyone, over and over,
that it would be alright

—apparently bought enough stuff from
jeff bezos to launch his penis to the moon.

—tweeted 473 tweets about how great I was doing
and how well everything was going.

—grieved and grieved every time a new name
was added to my pandemic death List,
counted the various degrees of separation between me
and dying
or not dying
but living forever with a new heart murmur.

—forgave myself for not writing poetry.

—tried to forgive myself for not writing poetry.

day 2 of moderna vaccine

has me wanting both to excise my left arm and the
entire front portion of my skull.

i have never appreciated the course weave of these
gray ikea sheets my husband loves so well for the deep
corner pockets.

i do not appreciate these sheets now except for
     the light
they block when pulled overhead. gray is the inside of
my mouth. my eyeballs. my lungs. my knees.

all we ever want is to not dwell here in this temporary
pain we've inflicted on ourselves and yet pain stretches
out time until it doesn't fit.

there is no way to discuss this without the whine.
i hear my own whimper and am ashamed.

in this gray bubble i've made for myself, cold cloth over
eyes, arm cradled across chest, all of this is to endure
the least now as possible.

i count 16 heartbeats in my temple. my husband may
be worse in his own careful cocoon next to me, but if
he rolls one more time and upsets the delicate balance
i have achieved, i will wish him dead alongside me.

pandemic is a 4-letter word

i have wished upon a facebook post
never to have known my family as I know them now,
arguing across a divide
where we forget we are related
for the principle of the thing.

a 4-letter word called mask
and vaxx
and hoax.
who knew how far up
a 6-inch cotton swab could reach?

we don't even speak the same language anymore.
kin has become epithet.

i want only to still believe that we,
as beings inhabiting this planet,
are salvageable,
that we have the dust of the cosmos
to guide our emergence,
and there is no worse corruption of the flesh than
    self-ish
my shadowself now squelched smaller than a mustard
    seed,
to constantly seek reassurances
thru the veil of my own confirmation bias.
that I am wrong about all this.

i want to be wrong about all this.
pandemic is a 4-letter word
we toss out the window
at the passing pick-up truck
driven by our probable neighbor that
called the hoa when we put out that
welcome to all sign in our yard.
he might even be a cousin.

Go back to 39.

a moth triptych

1

there was that time she was a moth
trapped between the glass and screen
of a 12-story-up window.
a great Polyphemus moth,
she could not have truly fit between,
flapping and patting her wings against the slide,
until finally she put her head on the cool track
and became something else,
always becoming something else
and stepped onto a shore of glass pebbles made of
    purple sand.
be the sunrise, she said, in her mouth-less form,
    be the spell.

2

i think of that moment between breaking down
    and emerging form,
when the moth is pupa-flavored soup in the cocoon.
and I wonder, does she taste the morning with no
    tongue,
smell sound and feel the world's beating heart,
know that the whole of her life is spent becoming
    something else?

3

her wings emerge damp in the wet of what she leaves
    behind.
she is the push and pull of moonlight,
the scent and sound of twilight wind.
she will taste the flavor of every flower in her feet…
and slide beneath the soil to become something else,
something new beneath the crescent moon.

mad baby*

1

when your first baby was very small,
brand new and wrinkled with dark hair
spiked all over her head,
every cry was a stab,
a frantic beckoning that meant
obligation
and desperation
and so much fear.

> *can I do this?*
> *what if I mess up?*
> *what if she is broken?*
> *check if she's still breathing—*
> *what does she need?*
> *give her what she needs,*
> *don't mess this up,*
> *keep her alive,*
> *keep her fed*
> *and dry*
> *and content,*
> *don't ever let anything bad happen to her*
> *ever,*
> *oh god I can't do this,*
> *i've already failed*
> *and she's barely here.*

2

today you learn that the painting you've been calling
    mad baby,
the painting that has grumped at you nearly every
    day this week,
is named after mike mctigue, the cyclonic celt,
light heavyweight boxing champion of the world
    from 1923-1925.
you especially love that like russel crowe fighting
    around the world,
painter george luks died not entirely unexpectedly
    after a bar brawl,
and this, my friends, this circle of mad baby and
    boxer and bar brawl,
is a poem.

3

by the time the second baby arrived,
barely a football in your arms,
you found her fury tender,
funny, proof-of-life wonderful
and never took it too seriously,
because you at least knew that you could
feed her
change her diapers
wipe her butt and her drooly mouth
and cuddle her close
and crying was only a small problem you had to solve

* from mike mcteague (1921) by george luks (1867-1933), part of the
permanent collection of the wichita art museum

instar*

there was that time you were nothing but mouth,
hungry searching devouring,
nothing but emptiness and the incessant need to
    be filled.
you are still that mouth,
muted,
furious,
lips sewn shut and unshut so that only certain things
    can come in and out of that cavern.
nothing tastes like you remember,
smell me in the moonlight
and cast out doubt and blame;
you are fat and way past forty.
remember that time you hated your mother and were
    afraid you were becoming your mother.
and you have been on this journey toward whatever
    you are today
for a very long time.
now you are mouth and wing and feet that taste
    the sky.

**caterpillar stage of development*

family dinner*

we have not yet earned a space at the grown-up table
with a grown-up glass of chianti,
have not yet learned the dynamic of aunt cybil,
the first to martyr herself on the folding chair,
or the discipline of uncle jack at the end.

that spot at the grown-up table will become yours
when great uncle leo passes,
when you finally get your period.

you will realize that sitting at the grown-up table
was a lot less fun than you had imagined,
even if everyone drinks,
that despite your age you're expected to still sit and be
    silent,
still expected to have no opinion save for the quiet
    solicitation
where you are expected to recite all of your
    accomplishments,
evidence their investment in you as f-a-m-i-l-y will
    pay off.

later when forming your own table
you will remember the special-occasion linens,
might purchase slightly more comfortable folding chairs,
will wonder if the table is long enough
or if you'll need to have your own children's table.

you will find yourself
in your own house,
sitting at the children's table,
so that your own will be more comfortable,
won't whine about not getting to sit at the adult table,
will ensure that food goes in mouths [mostly],
won't really mind that you're back at this table instead
    of that one.

**family Dinner (1985) by james r. bartz (1945–   ), part of the permanent
collection of the wichita art museum*

on why I am not a painter*

with apologies to Frank O'Hara

because I am a poet and not an artist
because words are hard but paint is harder
because when I draw a horse it looks like a giraffe
because I get lost in sound as often as I get lost in
    image
because I live in my head and not on the page
or maybe I mean that I don't think in pictures
because notebook paper is cheap and so is ink
        but BFK is a racket
because words can be thrown away
or rescued from the trash
because painting is expensive and messy
and stains make me feel like chaos,
but then so do poorly written sentences.
because somebody told me I shouldn't be a writer,
and we're all a little contrary that way.

*with a nod to the oranges, no 1 (black crows) (1952) by grace hartigan, in
response to frank o'hara's poetry, specifically on why i am not a painter.*

we mothers and sisters

multitaskers on rooftops,
minding babies and laundry,
mending and meals.
we play and sing,
clap and hum,
always.
no matter the air quality,
or the life you think we should have.
we live and die on rooftops,
raising our children along the way.

based on ring around the chimney (1939) by lawrence beall smith (1909-1995)

liner note 8

when johnny cash was my dad.

about the time rick ruban relaunched johnny cash's
career, i rediscovered cash in a $2 record bin at the
local dav. i had this old portable record player—why do
songs like "hey porter" always sound better when read
by a needle? why do the scratches and dust and skips
make everything sound like it was supposed to sound?

i decided johnny cash could've been my dad.

it's not that i didn't know who my dad was. i just decided
i could pick a better one, and, despite being grown and
knowing better, i adopted him.

i read his biographies and his autobiographies.
    i listened
to his interviews. i pretended to say grace at the table
with him. i also pretended that june and i went way
back. and when she died, i knew he would follow.

johnny cash's cover of "hurt"

the stories we tell ourselves come true

you have told this story before and you will tell this
    story again,
but there was this one time,
many one times,
where you were helpless.
you know that we are all helpless on the road to dying.
but sometimes when we are living,
we can't live all the way because someone else doesn't
        want us to,
won't let us,
or we're just crowded in by everybody else.

this time when you tell the story, you were stronger
    than you really were.
you didn't die back there in the closet
            –instar–
            on your way to becoming something else.
this time when you tell the story, you'll rewrite a
    triumphant ending,
one where you didn't hang yourself
but walked out this time,
past him and his red-veined forehead,
past him through the dark hallway,
and you'll emerge into the light of the front porch
to a rainbow halcyon sky
            –too much?–

when you tell this story again, you'll remind yourself
    to step around
the piles of hangers on the floor,
        over the guitar strings and forbidden books
    you told no one you read.

you'll add a faithful companion,
a cat that will follow you loyally into the sunlight,
where you'll grow wings,
        we'll all grow wings,
                and we'll fly away.

cloudscape

1

you argue with her about where exactly the sky
begins, if it has an invisible floor or if the part where
we stand has an invisible ceiling,

she points, assured, "the sky starts just above that
tree," the catalpa at the end of the block, a giant with
broad leaves shading even the second story of the
biggest house in the neighborhood.

is it where the sky begins or where the air turns blue,
or are we sure it doesn't begin at her knee? you ask
and probe to see where her certainty stops,

but she is adamant and assured that she knows exactly
where the boundary begins.

2

we worship the sky in kansas, the weather our weekly
liturgy, stare up to decide how long we have before
the storm breaks, before the rain falls, live just on the
edge of the sky's glory, and it is by her leave that we
are graced with skies so wide and clear, sometimes
see the tornado coming hours before in the eerie
premonition of green.

we hold on to cloud names, stare up for hours, look
for the faces of our grandfathers, the silhouettes of
cats and houses and dragons, stay huddled on the
porch to watch the lightning dance at night.

3

for four days you have thought about those people who
voluntarily got into their own coffin, the experimental
submersible built by hubris and too much money, that
while we worship wealth and consumption, there is
apparently a line we've drawn when too much money
means you don't deserve to live.

4

the first time you remember seeing mountains, you
must've driven for hours before your arrival, have no
memory of them getting closer. perhaps you were
napping from the backseat of your aunt's car, pulled
awake by some turn of the vehicle, some change in the
atmosphere.

the first time you remember seeing the mountains, you
lost breath and thought and substance and became
cloud and moist air and song lyric without tune, knew
the terror of falling out of the car down into the far
green-leaf valley floor hundreds of feet below, although
you never actually fell.

the first time you saw mountains you knew that's where
god lived, where he slept and held court and played
with the clouds and you wondered if you would ever
grow big enough to not be scared.

5

whole seasons walled and released leaving behind
the carved canyons, the memory of waters of
constellations of stones that never were. i have movies
that hold more substance than memories.

6

when my first was born, i had twins although i didn't
know it, that i'd bring home two shadows along with
the baby, shadows sliding to the floor to walk with us,
faithful as dogs. i grew anxiety and worry as surely as i
grew my daughter, who knew that i could grow terror
from a seed.

7

i smoked every day of my life from 17 to 29, we
counted cigarettes and pennies and scrounged for
long butts in ashtrays in ways that make my postcovid
brain spasm.

watching smokers now on television is porn, evoking
the smell and taste, yellow-stained fingertips.

i think I'm writing about air. air and death and memory
with the same substantial materials as an idea…

8

we have both decided that the sky begins at our feet,
that we are stardust and cosmos flakes, so of course
we live in the sky as celestial selves, in the bubble of
our island home.

poem as self-portrait 1265

this number is a fake number like all approximations,
based on some imaginary memory that feels as real as
time and as solid as a river

i will attempt to see without the imposition of
     external
gaze and will fail because I am only here as a reaction
to you, a mirror shadow.

i will attempt to see myself as a sum of disparate parts,
greater than the whole but parts blurry, smeared, and
gummy putty, fix-a-hole.

be honest and lie to myself.

the poems about moths and mouths and rapacious
starfish are still all poems about me.

enneagram 6 & enfj, know thyself, cancer, i am the
universe's version of shelter-in-place, succulent sweet
meat.

*untitled (self-portrait) (1910), peggy
nichols 1884-1941, permanent
collection of the wichita art museum

you dreamed so hard it felt like permanence

1

i dreamed a soft kitten cradled in my palm,
        soft and dying or nearly dead,
          found in a burrow beneath
the mower.
she cupped her paw over mine,
        created this warm den between us,

she prayed,
dear heavenly father,
we come to you in praise and ask,
if it be your will,
to either take the breath from this creature or give
    her life,
to not let her dwell in this heart-wrenching
    in-between,
lord,
but to take her quickly and mercifully
or let her live strongly,
in your precious name lord jesus,

and my palm began to sweat around that tiny fragile
    creature
        and I felt the inhalation,
         thought I believed in miracles,
          waited for the tiny mew,

felt the little body take a deep breath,

and then she exhaled her way to death,
        there in the palm of my beseeching hand.

2

it wasn't a kitten, he says. he's adamant it was a puppy,
white with brown spots, a puppy he brought home after
finding the litter under a porch, that the other puppies
with tails wagging and legs working had been dropped
off at a shelter, but this one, this one wasn't long for
the world and the shelter wouldn't take him and so he
brought that little puppy home to die in his hands so at
least he wouldn't be alone.

3

one time you dreamed the family cat named sara
had caught a wren in the yard,

an olympic leap of surprise and pounce and twist.
down came that mouthful of bird.

you dreamed you were the cat for a moment,
the flutter of tiny bird heart trapped,
crunched with glee down on the battering wing,

but then you were there to watch your mother rescue
    that bird,
chase the cat away with the hose, pick the bird up in
    her hand,

and you dreamed there would be a shoebox with soft
    swaddles,
coaxing feed into the bird.

but then she placed the palm of one hand over the
    other,
        creating a warm nest,
            the sudden startling jerk like a cat's leap
                as she cracked the bird's neck,
a handful of feathers left behind.

you can't let them suffer, she said.

invisible conversations

there was that time you remembered invisible
    conversations
with loved ones you haven't met yet,
remembered the glass he held full of ice chips and
    bourbon,
the scent strong and familiar and safe.

there was that time you compared scars that
would land like words in the body,
the smile lines you hoped to achieve, that
graceful gray swoop like water in his hairline,

remembered the comfort of his hand and what it
    might feel like
in a future you remember as clear as yesterday's
    breakfast.

we flow forward and back alone,
but flow we do,
riding our spaceship bodies through their slow slide to
    decay.

we attempt, we offer, to share space more closely,
to tell you what we taste inside,
our future selves and versions of our past selves
overlapping like blurry film.

there was that time you invented language,
tried to put together morphemes and sounds—
    restidudinal
    flaxion
    lem
made up words that mean nothing,
just flutter around attempting to push out and spread
    wings and fly.

there's no word for future memory,
something you dream so real and grieve when it
    doesn't happen
hasn't happened
might never happen.
i cannot remember all the lives i've lived
or will live in this body.

liner note 8

some of you Lindas jumped here first, just to be
contrary and see if this was the actual ending or if the
ending was buried somewhere further in [try page 62
or 66 for alternative endings].

telling your own story in the middle of discovering
the concern of (or rather, in the middle of being
    concerned
about) whether or not you even have a story to tell,
while also recovering from someone else's version of
the story, this is the heart of poetry. But it's also the
chaos and mess of living a life full of joy, sorrow,
grief, and love.

i also need to extend a big thank you—the artwork
here is from my time as the writer in residence at the
wichita art museum. i got to know some of the pieces
with an intimacy i never expected, and i was surprised
repeatedly by where my mind chose to dwell during my
time there. if you get the chance to visit the collection
in person, i highly encourage you to do so.

with gratitude…

Mother, wife, teacher, poet. **April Pameticky** shares time between roles as public school educator and peer facilitator within the creative community of artists and writers in Kansas. She launched the *Wichita Broadside Project* and has served as editor of *Voices of Kansas,* an online poetry journal focused on the youth of Kansas, sponsored by the Kansas Association for Teachers of English, for which she has also served as a board member since 2013. Her collaboration with photographer Amanda Pfister, *She Cast her Gaze,* has been at Steckline Gallery, the Ulrich Museum of Art, and the Johnson-Humrickshouse Museum in Ohio. She is currently a doctoral student at Kansas State University, studying teacher efficacy and the advent of AI technology as it affects writing pedagogy and methods in the secondary classroom.

This project was made possible, in part, by generous support from the Osage Arts Community.

Osage Arts Community provides temporary time, space and support for the creation of new artistic works in a retreat format, serving creative people of all kinds — visual artists, composers, poets, fiction and nonfiction writers. Located on a 152-acre farm in an isolated rural mountainside setting in Central Missouri and bordered by ¾ of a mile of the Gasconade River, OAC provides residencies to those working alone, as well as welcoming collaborative teams, offering living space and workspace in a country environment to emerging and mid-career artists. For more information, visit us at www.osageac.org

www.ingramcontent.com/pod-product-compliance
Lightning Source LLC
Chambersburg PA
CBHW031310130726
47988CB00007B/2789